Copyright © 2023 by Trient Press

All rights reserved. No part of this publication may be reproduced, distributed, or transmitted in any form or by any means, including photocopying, recording, or other electronic or mechanical methods, without the prior written permission of the publisher, except in the case of brief quotations embodied in critical reviews and certain other noncommercial uses permitted by copyright law. For permission requests, write to the publisher, addressed "Attention: Permissions Coordinator," at the address below.

Criminal copyright infringement, including infringement without monetary gain, is investigated by the FBI and is punishable by up to five years in federal prison and a fine of $250,000.

Except for the original story material written by the author, all songs, song titles, and lyrics mentioned in the novel From Data to Disruption: How AI is Changing Business Forever are the exclusive property of the respective artists, songwriters, and copyright holder.

Trient Press
3375 S Rainbow Blvd
#81710, SMB 13135
Las Vegas,NV 89180

Ordering Information:
Quantity sales. Special discounts are available on quantity purchases by corporations, associations, and others. For details, contact the publisher at the address above.
Orders by U.S. trade bookstores and wholesalers. Please contact Trient Press: Tel: (775) 996-3844; or visit www.trientpress.com.

Printed in the United States of America

Publisher's Cataloging-in-Publication data
Trient Press
A title of a book : Trientrepreneur

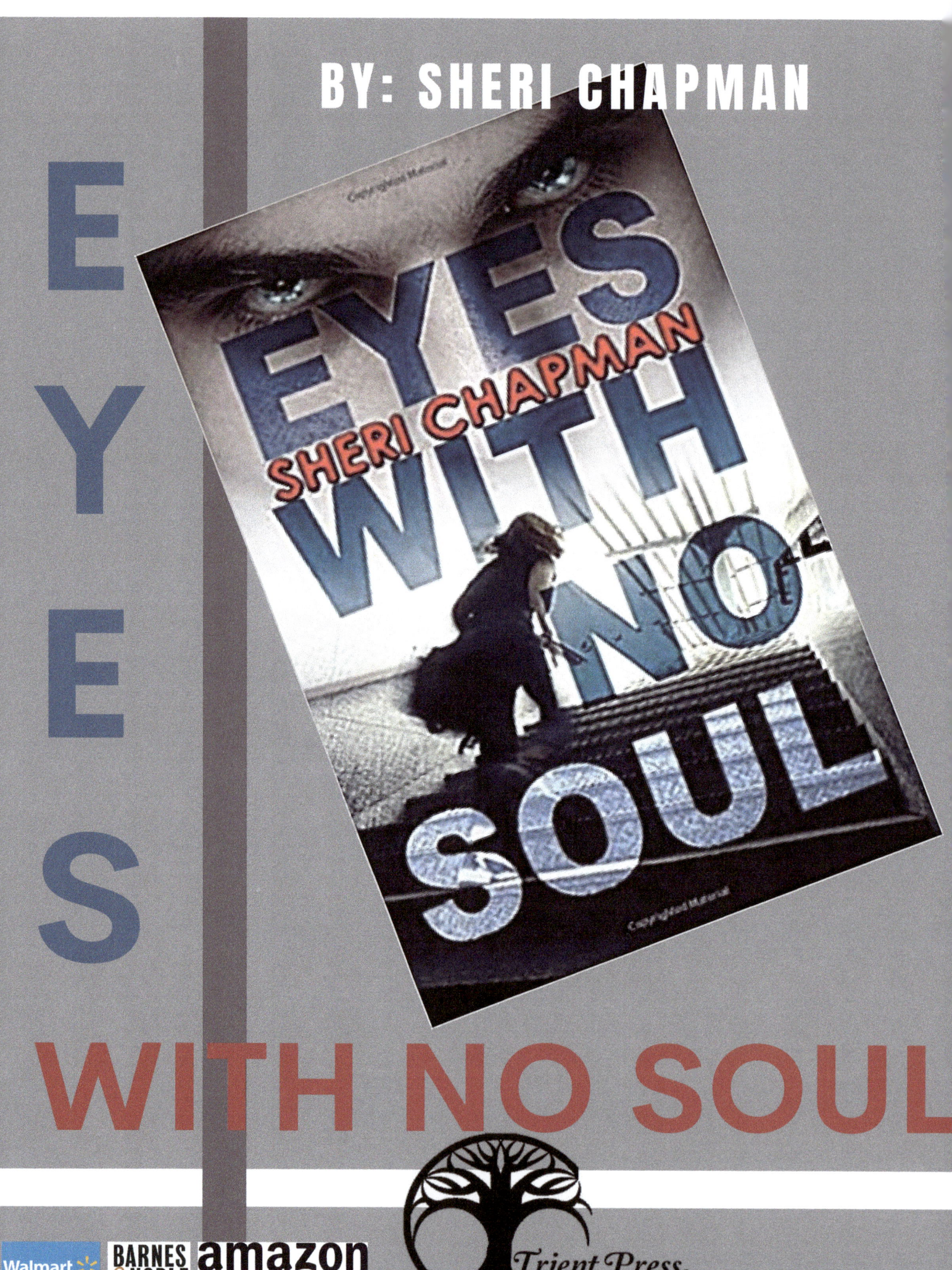

AUTHOR TIPS: 06

- Author Tips
- Nurturing Your Narrative: Growth Strategies
- Spring Into Action: Refreshing Your Writing Routine
- Unlocking Creativity: A Month-Long Exploration of Effective Writing Routines
- Cultivating Characters: Developing Depth and Relatability
- Engaging with Your Literary Garden: Cultivating an Audience and Growing Your Presence

COVER FEATURE: Jim Lutes
Unleash Your Potential: Inside the Mind and Master of Personal and Professional Success   31

TABLE OF CONTENTS
RIENTREPRENEUR
ISSUE 18

Editor-in-Chief
Head Staff-Writer
Melisa Ruscsak

Managing Editor
Graphic Design Editor
Staff Writer
Kristina Wenzl-Figueroa

ECONOMICS SECTION: 35

- Global Economic Outlook for 2024: Navigating Trends, Challenges, and Opportunities
- Financial Well-Being: Cultivating your economic garden
- The Impact of Remote Work: Urban Economies
- Global Economic Blossoming: Emerging markets to watch

TECH SECTION: 46

- AI Innovations & Their Impact on Industries
- Fortifying the Digital Frontier: Strategic Cybersecurity in the Contemporary Business Landscape
- Innovative Horizons: San Diego's Tech Entrepreneurs Catalyzing Growth
- Quantum Horizons: Unveiling the Future Through Quantum Computing

TRAVEL SECTION: 56

- Springtime Escapes: Exploring Entrepreneurial Inspiration Around the Globe
- Discovering Entrepreneurial Spring: A Journey of Innovation and Inspiration
- Unveiling Spring's Hidden Gems: Quirky Destinations for the Adventurous Traveler
- Run for the Roses: Exploring the Timeless Tradition of the Kentucky Derby
- Recipes

OFF THE PATH
How To Get Your Life Off The Road Of Failure

Tierell Goodman

In *Off The Path*, Tierell Goodman shares his astonishing life story and reveals that most of us face various personal battles internally and as if there is no way out.

Goodman's inspiration of no hold bar mentalit and no more excuses to push past the storm of life, eliminates self-doubt and negative people.

To be able to reach our full potential, accepting and building self-love, viewing life through untinted glasses, and developing a relationship with God, get us to where each of us were designed to be

TIERELL GOODMAN

Trient Press

TRIENT PRESS MAGAZINE APRIL/ MAY

AUTHOR TIPS
"20 Essential Tips for Aspiring Authors: A Guide to Writing Success"

1. Read widely and voraciously to expand your understanding of different writing styles and techniques.
2. Set aside dedicated time for writing each day to maintain consistency and discipline.
3. Experiment with different genres and formats to find your unique voice and niche.
4. Keep a notebook or digital file handy to jot down ideas and inspirations whenever they strike.
5. Edit ruthlessly - cut unnecessary words and phrases to make your writing clear and concise.
6. Join writing groups or communities for support, feedback, and networking opportunities.
7. Don't be afraid to write poorly in your first drafts; perfection comes through revision.
8. Embrace rejection as a natural part of the writing journey and use feedback to improve.
9. Study the craft of storytelling, including plot structure, character development, and pacing.
10. Take breaks and allow yourself time to rest and recharge creatively.
11. Practice empathy to create authentic and relatable characters and situations.
12. Find a writing routine that works for you, whether it's early morning sessions or late-night marathons.
13. Attend writing workshops, conferences, and literary events to learn from seasoned authors and industry professionals.
14. Balance self-expression with audience engagement; consider your readers' interests and perspectives.
15. Don't compare your progress or success to others; focus on your own growth and journey.
16. Cultivate resilience and perseverance to overcome setbacks and challenges.
17. Experiment with different writing tools and software to find what enhances your productivity and creativity.
18. Read your work aloud to catch awkward phrasing, errors, and inconsistencies.
19. Develop a strong opening hook to grab readers' attention from the start.
20. Celebrate your achievements, no matter how small, to stay motivated and inspired on your writing journey.

Whether you're a novice writer seeking guidance or a seasoned author looking for a refresher, this comprehensive list of tips is your roadmap to honing your craft, overcoming obstacles, and achieving writing success.

> **The worst enemy to creativity is self-doubt**
>
> — SYLVIA PLAT

Quit doubting yourself.
You've got what it takes.

Give us a call today.

~Now accepting all genres~

1-775-996-3844

ARE YOU HAPPY

M.L. Ruscsak

Trient Press

TRIENT PRESS MAGAZINE   APRIL/ MAY

NURTURING YOUR NARRATIVE:
Growth Strategies

BY: JIM LUTES

In the world of writing, where the personal and the professional intricately intertwine, authors continually seek methods to refine their craft and deepen their connection with readers. One profound source of inspiration and strategy can be found in the teachings of Jim Lutes, a renowned figure in the realms of personal development and business psychology. Lutes' approaches to self-improvement and strategic thinking offer a treasure trove of techniques that authors can adapt to foster growth in their writing and establish a more profound engagement with their audience.

Understanding Jim Lutes' Philosophies:
At the core of Jim Lutes' philosophies lies the emphasis on the power of the mind and the potential for transformation through intentional thought and action. He advocates for creating a robust mental framework that fosters resilience, creativity, and adaptability—qualities essential for any author aspiring to resonate with their readers and thrive in the dynamic landscape of literature.

Applying Mindset Strategies to Writing:

Cultivating a Growth Mindset: Lutes encourages individuals to embrace a growth mindset, a perspective that views challenges as opportunities for development rather than insurmountable obstacles. Authors can adopt this mindset to persevere through writing blocks, critical feedback, and the ever-present fear of inadequacy. Viewing each writing project as a chance to evolve not only enhances the quality of one's work but also builds resilience in the face of the publishing industry's uncertainties.

Visualization Techniques:
Visualization is a potent tool in Lutes' arsenal, enabling individuals to manifest their goals through focused and detailed mental imagery. Authors can leverage this strategy to envision their narrative arc, character development, or even the impact they wish their work to have on readers, thereby bringing a clearer focus and intentionality to their writing process.

AUTHOR TIPS |TRIENT PRESS

Strategic Goal Setting: Lutes underscores the importance of setting clear, actionable goals. For authors, this means defining not only what they want to achieve with their writing—be it to inform, entertain, or provoke thought—but also setting specific milestones for their writing process, such as completing a chapter a week or dedicating time to refine their style.

Building a Connection with the Audience:
Authenticity: One of Jim Lutes' key tenets is authenticity—being true to oneself. In writing, this translates to finding one's voice and staying true to it, a practice that not only enhances personal satisfaction but also fosters a genuine connection with readers who seek truth and relatability in literature.

Building a Connection with the Audience:
Authenticity: One of Jim Lutes' key tenets is authenticity—being true to oneself. In writing, this translates to finding one's voice and staying true to it, a practice that not only enhances personal satisfaction but also fosters a genuine connection with readers who seek truth and relatability in literature.

Understanding the Audience:
Just as Lutes tailors his strategies to the needs and aspirations of his followers, authors should strive to understand their readers' desires, fears, and motivations. This empathetic approach can inform the themes, characters, and narratives authors choose to explore, making their work more resonant and impactful.

Engagement:
Lutes' ability to engage his audience is paramount to his impact; similarly, authors must consider how to engage readers actively. This might involve crafting compelling openings, weaving interactive elements into their narratives, or engaging with readers through social media or literary events, thereby creating a community around their work.

In conclusion, Jim Lutes' strategies for personal and professional growth offer invaluable insights for authors seeking to nurture their narratives and deepen their audience connection. By internalizing and applying these principles, writers can not only enhance their craft but also embark on a more fulfilling and resonant literary journey. As authors integrate these growth strategies into their practice, they not only evolve their narratives but also contribute to the rich tapestry of human experience and understanding, one story at a time.

> **Strategic Goal Setting:**
> Lutes underscores the importance of setting clear, actionable goals. For authors, this means defining not only what they want to achieve with their writing—be it to inform, entertain, or provoke thought—but also setting specific milestones for their writing process, such as completing a chapter a week or dedicating time to refine their style.

What if your mother move far away with you? What i she hid you away from? Would you wonder why

This is the lifelong dilemm Bob Rebertson must resolve.

At only fifteen years old, h wants to protect his mother. But lately he wonders who's protecting who- and from what?

After a life-altering conversation with his mother, he's thrown headlong into place of dream, death, destruction, and salvation - a place connected to our world in ways he could never imagine. He meets new friends, battles vicious enemies, and has his resolve tested at each step of the journey as he searches for the truth.

But attaining that truth may spell disaster for everyone he cares for.

TINA Maurine

intense. passionate. unforgettable.

TRIENT PRESS MAGAZINE   APRIL/ MAY

Spring into Action:
REFRESHING YOUR WRITING ROUTINE

As winter's chill wanes and the vivacious hues of spring beckon, there lies a perfect opportunity for authors to rejuvenate their writing routines. The essence of spring—renewal, growth, and vitality—can infuse new energy into your creative endeavors. Embracing this season of transformation can lead to profound advancements in your work and well-being. Here's how you can align your writing practice with the vitality of spring, setting fresh goals, embracing the outdoors, and drawing inspiration from nature's resurgence.

SETTING NEW GOALS:

Reflect and Reassess:

Begin by reflecting on past achievements and challenges. Assess what aspects of your writing routine have served you well and which require modification. Use this insight to set clear, attainable goals for the upcoming season. Whether it's completing a manuscript, enhancing your style, or exploring new genres, let your objectives mirror spring's promise of growth.

Create a Goal Ladder:

Break down your overarching goals into smaller, manageable steps, akin to a plant's gradual growth. Establish monthly, weekly, and daily milestones to maintain momentum and track progress, allowing each completed task to propel you forward.

Public Commitment:

Share your goals with a writing group, mentor, or on social media. Making your intentions public can enhance accountability and provide a support network to encourage you along your journey.

AUTHOR TIPS | TRIENT PRESS

EMBRACING OUTDOOR WRITING SESSIONS:

Scheduled Retreats:

Plan regular outdoor writing retreats. Even a few hours at a local nature reserve or a day spent by a lakeside can provide a significant boost to your creative output, offering new sights, sounds, and experiences to fuel your imagination.

Nature as Your Office:

With the warmer weather and longer days, take your writing outdoors. Whether it's a park, garden, or your backyard, fresh air and natural surroundings can stimulate creativity and offer a refreshing change of scenery.

Mobilize Your Tools:

Equip yourself with a portable writing kit—notebooks, laptop, pens, and perhaps a voice recorder for capturing spontaneous ideas. Ensure you have a comfortable, portable seat or find a welcoming bench or café with outdoor seating.

USING NATURE AS INSPIRATION:

Photographic Inspiration:

Capture images of your outdoor escapades. These can serve as visual prompts or settings for your stories, or simply evoke the mood and atmosphere you wish to convey through your writing.

Themes of Renewal & Growth:

Let the themes of spring—rebirth, rejuvenation, and resilience—permeate your narratives or characters. Explore plots that mirror the cycle of renewal or characters that embody the resilience and vitality of the natural world.

Sensory Observations:

Engage all your senses to absorb the nuances of the natural world. Observe the budding flora, the bustling fauna, and the dynamic skies. Translate these observations into vivid descriptions, innovative metaphors, and dynamic settings in your writing.

Allowing the energy of spring to permeate your writing routine can lead to profound personal and professional growth. By setting new goals, integrating the outdoors into your creative process, and drawing inspiration from nature, you can invigorate your practice and imbue your writing with the freshness, dynamism, and vibrancy of the season. Embrace this time of renewal to cultivate a deeper connection with your craft and nurture your narrative's growth.

Unlocking Creativity:
A Month-Long Exploration of Effective Writing Routines

In the cacophony of everyday life, finding the rhythm that harmonizes with our creative impulses can be a daunting task. For writers, this pursuit of an effective routine is not merely about time management—it's a quest for the elusive balance between discipline and inspiration. Welcome to a month-long journey dedicated to unraveling the mysteries of effective writing routines.

Over the next four weeks, we will embark on a structured exploration, delving into the intricacies of crafting a routine that not only sparks creativity but also sustains productivity. From reflecting on our current habits to experimenting with techniques favored by literary luminaries, each day will offer a new opportunity to hone our craft and unlock our potential.

Join us as we navigate the labyrinth of words, seeking the elusive formula for a writing routine that works.

AUTHOR TIPS |TRIENT PRESS

TRIENT PRESS MAGAZINE　　　　　　　APRIL/ MAY

Week 1: Discovering Your Ideal Routine

Embark on a journey of self-discovery this week as you delve into the realm of writing routines. Start by reflecting on your current habits and discern what's effective and what's not. Take cues from accomplished authors, exploring their routines for inspiration.

Experiment with different writing times, from early mornings to late evenings, and test various methods like the pomodoro technique. Engage in long, uninterrupted sessions to gauge your productivity. By week's end, reflect on your experiences to identify the strategies that resonate most with you.

Week 2: Crafting Your Personal Writing Routine

Armed with insights from the previous week, dive into the process of crafting a personalized writing routine. Set clear, achievable goals and carve out a dedicated writing space. Schedule daily time blocks, incorporating breaks and rewards to maintain momentum. Ease into your sessions with outlining or brainstorming, and eliminate distractions for focused writing. By week's end, review and refine your routine to optimize your productivity.

TRIENT PRESS MAGAZINE APRIL/ MAY

MONTH OVERVIEW: EFFECTIVE WRITING ROUTINES EXPLORATION: WEEKS 1 & 2

Week 1: Discovering Your Ideal Routine
- Day 1: Reflect on your current routine and identify what's working and what's not.
- Day 2: Research the writing routines of successful authors and note appealing strategies.
- Day 3: Experiment with a morning writing session.
- Day 4: Try an evening writing session.
- Day 5: Test a short burst (pomodoro) writing method—25 minutes writing, 5 minutes break.
- Day 6: Engage in a long, uninterrupted writing session.
- Day 7: Reflect on the week and identify what felt most productive.

Week 2: Crafting Your Personal Writing Routine
- Day 8: Set clear, achievable writing goals for the week.
- Day 9: Create a dedicated writing space.
- Day 10: Schedule daily writing time blocks based on last week's insights.
- Day 11: Implement breaks and rewards into your routine.
- Day 12: Use the first 15 minutes to outline or brainstorm to ease into writing.
- Day 13: Write with all distractions removed (phone off, internet off).
- Day 14: Review and adjust your routine based on this week's experiences.

AUTHOR TIPS TRIENT PRESS

As we journey through the labyrinth of effective writing routines, guided by insights gleaned from weeks of self-discovery and experimentation, we find ourselves on the precipice of transformation. Weeks 1 and 2 have been a revelation—a time of reflection, exploration, and refinement. We've delved deep into the nuances of our writing habits, drawing inspiration from the routines of literary giants and crafting personalized strategies to fuel our creativity. Now, as we stand at the threshold of

Weeks 3 and 4, we embark on the next leg of our journey—a journey fraught with challenges yet ripe with opportunities for growth. In the coming weeks, we will confront the specter of writer's block head-on, armed with newfound insights and resilience. We will navigate the turbulent waters of productivity, seeking to maintain momentum and drive towards our goals. Join us as we delve deeper into the heart of the writing process, propelled by the knowledge gained from our past experiences and fueled by the promise of what lies ahead.

Week 3: Tackling Writer's Block

This week, confront the nemesis of all writers: writer's block. Identify its triggers and experiment with various strategies to overcome it. Embrace free writing or journaling to kickstart your creativity, and change your environment to stimulate fresh ideas.

Seek inspiration from reading and discussions with peers. Break down daunting tasks into manageable chunks and reflect on what tactics prove most effective in combating writer's block.

MONTH OVERVIEW: EFFECTIVE WRITING ROUTINES EXPLORATION: WEEKS 3 & 4

Week 3: Tackling Writer's Block

- Day 15: Identify the triggers of your writer's block.
- Day 16: Try free writing or journaling to overcome inertia.
- Day 17: Change your environment (write in a café, library, park).
- Day 18: Read something inspiring or related to your writing project.
- Day 19: Discuss your ideas with a friend or fellow writer.
- Day 20: Break down your writing project into smaller, more manageable tasks.
- Day 21: Reflect on what strategies helped reduce your writer's block.

Week 4: Maintaining Productivity

- Day 22: Set up a system to track your writing progress (word count, pages, time spent).
- Day 23: Learn and apply a new productivity technique or tool.
- Day 24: Reward yourself for meeting a writing milestone.
- Day 25: Revisit your goals to ensure they remain SMART (Specific, Measurable, Achievable, Relevant, Time-bound).
- Day 26: Join or create a writing accountability group.
- Day 27: Schedule regular reviews of your writing progress and goals.
- Day 28: Plan a day off from writing to recharge and gain fresh perspectives.

TRIENT PRESS MAGAZINE — APRIL/ MAY

Week 4: Maintaining Productivity

As the month draws to a close, focus on sustaining your newfound productivity.

Establish systems to track your progress and explore new productivity techniques or tools.

Celebrate milestones and ensure your goals remain SMART.

Leverage the support of writing accountability groups and schedule regular reviews to stay on track.

Don't forget to remember to take breaks to recharge and gain fresh perspectives, ensuring a sustainable and fulfilling writing practice.

This month-long exploration of effective writing routines offers a structured approach to discovering, crafting, and maintaining a personalized routine that suits your unique preferences and schedule.

By integrating insights from successful authors and experimenting with various techniques, you can cultivate a productive and fulfilling writing practice. Regular reflection and adjustment ensure that your routine remains effective and sustainable, fostering creativity and consistency in your writing endeavors.

Trient Press

Trient Press Publishing

Here at Trient Press, our obvious goal is to put our authors' books in front of as many eyes as possible; to that end though, we do not value a book solely in sales. A book that sells a million copies is no more important than a title that sells only a hundred. Many books have a greater value in the message within the pages, than the bills it puts in our author's wallet. Aligned with this mindset, the authors we currently have often participate in charity anthologies, which all proceeds go to a selected non-profit or charity group.

Trient Basmak

Trient Besmak is set to be our International leg. Set In Instanbul, Turkey, we high expectations from this office. Adding translations from English to Turkish and vice versa. In addition to signing authors from the region.

We will be working with area prepsientives to distribute our current collection in the country while bringing the voices of the our new authors to our current markets.

Trient Press Printing & Distribution

Trient Printing and Distribution (TP&D) will focus on the printing of books, magazines and other media on-site, leading the way using mostly green-energy in its printing, cutting, and binding, while also keeping the carbon footprint below industry standards without cutting corners on quality or production speeds. Following the printing and binding, printed materials will then be entered directly into the distribution channel to be delivered to the ultimate reader or user.

Trient Evolve

Trient Evolve is set to be a marketing agency which will continue to partner with small business outreach. Continuing our work with D & Dragon Radio and Trientrepreneur Magazine. Dedicated to the sole purpose of helping small business a author in reaching their audience.

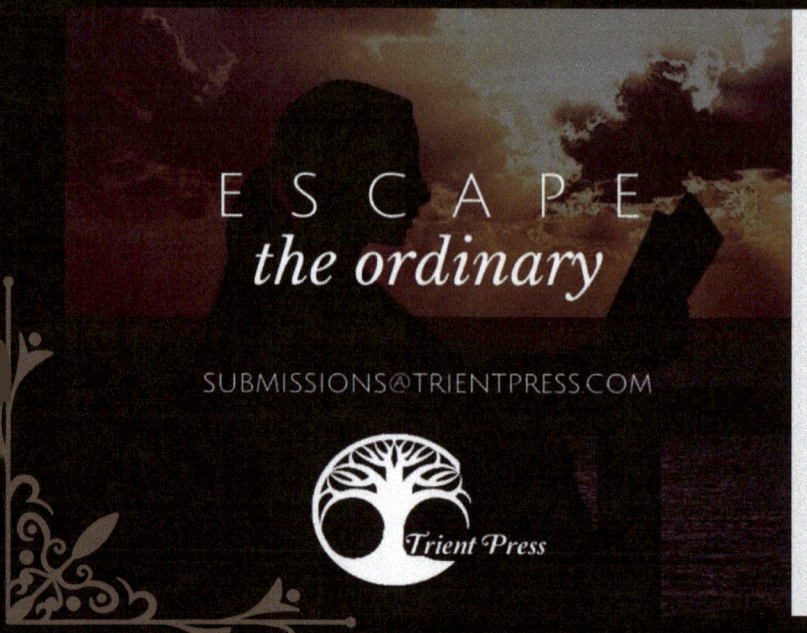

ESCAPE *the ordinary*

SUBMISSIONS@TRIENTPRESS.COM

Mission Statement

Since its conception, Trient Press has always been about more than just meeting author expectations, we've always aimed to exceed them.

Trient Press has a simple mission statement:

Trient Press is a publishing company focused on producing high-quality, ORIGINAL e-books, paperbacks, and hardcovers, which exceed our author clients' needs and goals.

We support creative, non-hateful expression across multiple fictional genres.
We care about your publishing success and will work tirelessly to meet your goals and get your book in the hands of readers everywhere.

1-775-996-3844

CULTIVATING CHARACTERS:
Developing Depth and Relatability

In the tapestry of narrative creation, characters are the vibrant threads that weave depth, emotion, and resonance into the story's fabric. As a novelist who has navigated the ebb and flow of countless plots and personas, I've come to recognize the paramount importance of cultivating characters who are not merely figures on a page but living, breathing entities with whom readers can form profound connections. In the spirit of spring, a season emblematic of growth and renewal, let us delve into the art of character development, drawing parallels from nature's own process of transformation.

Sowing the Seeds of Characterization:

Just as a gardener meticulously selects seeds before planting, a writer must begin with the core essence of their characters. Start by defining their fundamental traits, values, and desires. Yet, remember, like seeds, these traits are merely the genesis of what is to be a dynamic growth process. Your characters should possess the potential to evolve, influenced by the plot's 'climate' and the 'soil' of their environment.

Nurturing with Experiences:

In nature, a plant's growth is influenced by its exposure to sunlight, water, and nutrients. Similarly, characters develop through their experiences. The trials they endure, the joys they savor, and the decisions they make all contribute to their growth. Craft situations that challenge your characters, compel them to confront their fears, or force them to question their beliefs. It is through these trials that they stretch toward the sunlight of their potential.

Pruning for Growth:

Just as a gardener prunes plants to remove dead or overgrown branches, a writer must sometimes refine characters by stripping away what is unnecessary or incongruent. This might mean revising traits that no longer fit, removing redundant characters who overshadow growth, or sharpening blurred edges of personality. Pruning ensures that your characters can grow more robust and more vibrant, resonating authenticity and depth.

Observing the Blossoming:

Patience is vital in both gardening and character development. Just as one cannot rush a flower to bloom, a character's growth should feel organic, not forced or hurried. Allow your characters to evolve at a pace that aligns with the story's rhythm, ensuring their transformation is believable and earned. Witnessing your characters blossom into their full complexity is one of the most gratifying experiences as an author.

Harvesting Relatability:

Ultimately, the goal is to cultivate characters that resonate with readers, characters who reflect the multifaceted nature of being human. Just as a gardener admires their blooms, relish in the characters you've nurtured. They should mirror the diversity of human experience, embodying strengths and flaws, certainties and doubts, growth and regressions.

Character development, much like the arrival of spring, is a process marked by transformation and renewal. It demands attention, patience, and a nuanced understanding of the elements that contribute to growth. By imbuing your characters with depth, ensuring they evolve authentically, and pruning them to their core essence, you create a narrative garden rich with realism and relatability. Just as the gardener stands back to admire their vibrant garden, so too can you revel in the world you've cultivated—one where characters live, breathe, and resonate with the palpable essence of life itself.

At Trient Evolve, we are committed to empowering entrepreneurs and business owners with cutting-edge solutions to drive growth, efficiency, and success in today's dynamic marketplace. Explore our comprehensive range of business solutions carefully curated to address the unique challenges and opportunities your business may encounter

TRIENT
EVOLVE

Engaging with Your Literary Garden:

Cultivating an Audience and Growing Your Presence

In the realm of literature, authors not only create worlds with words but also must tend to their literary garden—their audience. Like gardeners who nurture their plants, authors must cultivate their relationship with readers and the broader literary community to thrive. Here's how you can nurture your literary garden, ensuring it flourishes and sustains vibrant connections with your audience.

TRIENT PRESS MAGAZINE　　　　　　　　　　　　　　　　APRIL/ MAY

PLANTING SEEDS: ESTABLISHING YOUR PRESENCE

CREATE A ROBUST AUTHOR PLATFORM:

Develop a professional website and active social media profiles. These are the seeds of your garden, the basic elements where your presence can start to grow and where readers can find and engage with you.

CONSISTENT BRANDING:

Ensure your online presence and your publications have consistent branding. This makes you easily recognizable and helps to establish a strong, professional image.

START A BLOG OR NEWSLETTER:

Share your writing journey, insights into your process, and snippets of your work. Regular updates keep your audience engaged and offer them value, encouraging them to return and interact.

AUTHOR TIPS | TRIENT PRESS

TRIENT PRESS MAGAZINE   APRIL/ MAY

WATERING AND NURTURING: BUILDING RELATIONSHIPS & ESTABLISHING YOUR PRESENCE

ENGAGE ON SOCIAL MEDIA:

Don't just post; interact. Respond to comments, engage with readers' posts, and participate in literary discussions. Like watering your garden, this consistent engagement helps relationships with your audience grow.

COLLABORATE WITH OTHER AUTHORS:

Just as companion planting can help a garden thrive, working with other authors can introduce you to their audience and them to yours, fostering a supportive literary ecosystem.

ATTEND LITERARY EVENTS:

Whether in-person or virtual, participating in readings, book clubs, and other literary events allows you to connect with your audience and fellow authors, enriching your literary community.

TRIENT PRESS MAGAZINE APRIL/ MAY

PRUNING:
REFINING YOUR AUDIENCE ENGAGEMENT

GATHER FEEDBACK:

Use surveys, read reviews, and ask for reader input to understand what your audience enjoys and what they'd like to see from you. This feedback can guide you in tailoring your content and interactions.

FOCUS YOUR EFFORTS:

Over time, you'll learn which platforms and types of engagement yield the best results. Focus your energy there, rather than trying to be everywhere at once.

STAY AUTHENTIC:

As your audience grows, maintain the authentic voice and presence that attracted them to you in the first place. Authenticity is the key to long-lasting relationships.

AUTHOR TIPS | TRIENT PRESS

HARVESTING: REAPING THE REWARDS OF YOUR LITERARY GARDEN

READER LOYALTY:

A well-tended literary garden results in a loyal audience that looks forward to your work, attends your events, and supports your publications.

WORD-OF-MOUTH PROMOTION:

Engaged readers become your advocates, sharing their enthusiasm for your work with others and helping your audience grow.

SUSTAINED ENGAGEMENT:

Over time, your literary garden will sustain itself, with readers returning for each new work you produce and contributing to a self-perpetuating cycle of engagement and growth.

By nurturing your literary garden with attention, care, and genuine interaction, you can cultivate a thriving community of readers and fellow writers. This community will not only support your current works but will also be the fertile ground from which your future projects will bloom. Like any garden, it requires patience and persistence, but the rewards—a loyal audience and a robust presence in the literary community—are well worth the effort.

JIM LUTES

UNLEASH YOUR POTENTIAL:
~INSIDE THE MIND AND MASTER OF PERSONAL AND PROFESSIONAL SUCCESS~

In the ever-evolving landscape of personal development and entrepreneurial triumphs, few figures command as much reverence and admiration as Jim Lutes. Renowned for his mastery of the human mind and his ability to unlock untapped potential, Lutes stands as a beacon of inspiration for individuals seeking to transcend limitations and achieve extraordinary success. Through decades of relentless dedication and innovation, he has not only transformed lives but also reshaped the very fabric of how we perceive personal growth and professional achievement.

AUTHOR SPOTLIGHT | TRIENT PRESS

> "Give me your excuses so that I can incinerate them"

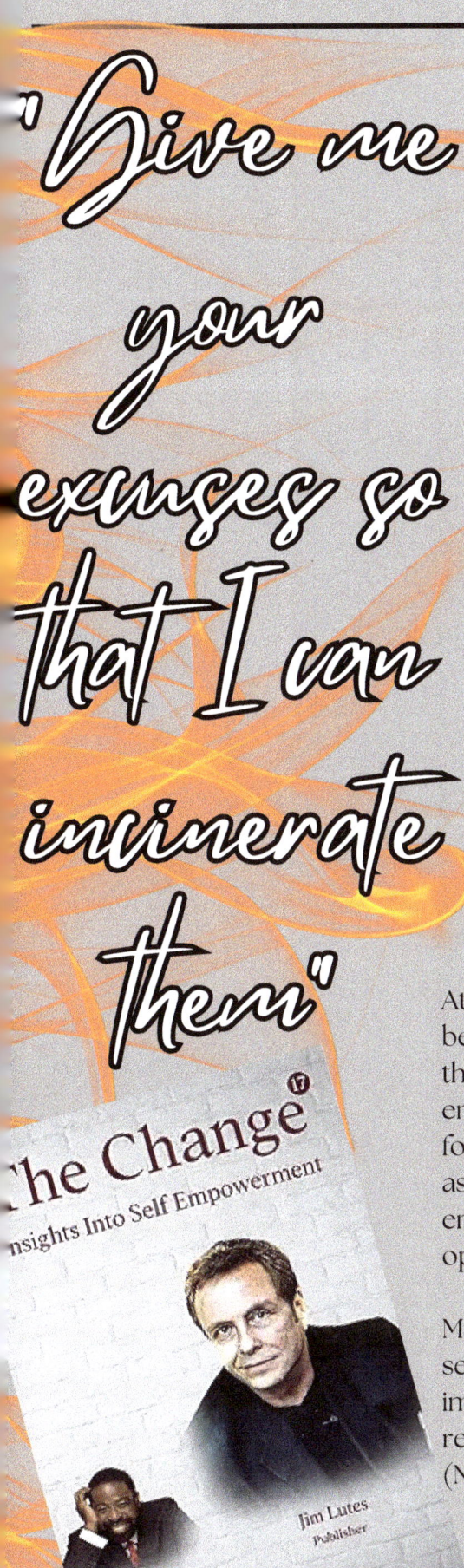

The Journey Unfolds: From Curiosity to Mastery

Jim Lutes' journey toward becoming a titan in the realms of personal development and motivational speaking is one marked by serendipity, determination, and unwavering passion. From his formative years, Lutes exhibited an insatiable curiosity for the intricacies of human behavior and the potential of the mind to shape destinies. This curiosity, nurtured by a foundational education in psychology and cognitive sciences, served as the catalyst for his eventual pivot toward a career dedicated to empowering others.

However, it was a transformative moment of realization that propelled Lutes onto his chosen path. Recognizing the profound impact of mindset and attitude on personal achievement, he embarked on a journey of self-discovery and mastery, immersing himself in the study of motivational psychology and performance enhancement. Through years of rigorous exploration and refinement, Lutes honed his expertise, emerging as a leading authority in leveraging the power of the mind for transformative change.

Philosophies That Forge Success

At the core of Jim Lutes' teachings lies a set of philosophies that serve as the bedrock for personal and professional success. Central to his approach is the belief in the inherent power of the mind to shape one's reality. Lutes emphasizes the importance of subconscious reprogramming, advocating for the alignment of subconscious patterns with one's goals and aspirations. He espouses the virtues of cultivating a growth mindset, encouraging individuals to embrace challenges and view setbacks as opportunities for growth.

Moreover, Lutes integrates the practice of visualization and strategic goal setting into his methodologies, enabling individuals to create vivid mental images of their desired outcomes and chart a clear path toward their realization. Through techniques such as Neuro-Linguistic Programming (NLP), cognitive-behavioral approaches, and mindfulness training, he equips individuals with the tools to overcome limiting beliefs, cultivate empowering thought patterns, and harness their cognitive resources more effectively.

Impact Across Diverse Arenas

Jim Lutes' influence extends far beyond the realm of personal coaching, permeating various sectors and industries with profound implications. In the world of entrepreneurship, his insights have revolutionized organizational cultures, fostering resilience, innovation, and accountability among leaders and teams alike. Through tailored coaching and consultancy services, he has guided countless businesses toward sustainable growth and success.

Similarly, in the arena of sports performance, Lutes has emerged as a trusted advisor, helping athletes optimize their mental game and achieve peak performance under pressure. By instilling confidence, focus, and resilience, he has empowered athletes to transcend their limitations and achieve extraordinary feats on the field of play.

A Legacy of Empowerment

Jim Lutes' professional achievements stand as a testament to his unwavering commitment to empowering individuals and organizations to reach their peak potential. From esteemed authorship to prestigious speaking engagements, from innovative programs to impactful collaborations, Lutes' legacy continues to inspire and guide generations toward greater success and fulfillment.

As he continues to evolve his offerings and extend his impact through innovative projects and events, Lutes remains dedicated to enhancing individual and organizational performance. From exclusive mastermind gatherings to focused deep dive sessions, he continues to shape the trajectories of individuals and organizations toward excellence, ensuring that his influence will continue to resonate for generations to come.

> **DON'T BE UPSET BY THE RESULTS YOU DIDN'T GET WITH THE WORK YOU DIDN'T DO.**

Conclusion: The Legacy Lives On

In conclusion, Jim Lutes' enduring legacy serves as a beacon of inspiration and guidance for those navigating the tumultuous waters of personal and professional development. Through his transformative philosophies and impactful methodologies, Lutes has left an indelible mark on the landscape of entrepreneurship and personal growth, ensuring that his influence will continue to resonate for generations to come.

To connect with Jim Lutes and explore his work further, follow his social media profiles and immerse yourself in the transformative journey toward personal and professional fulfillment.

AMPLIFY YOUR INFLUENCE AND EMPOWER YOUR JOURNEY
WITH ATS LEADS

WELCOME TO ATS LEADS – YOUR POWERHOUSE FOR ELEVATING YOUR IMPACT IN THE WORLD.

Your Ultimate Lead Generation Solution! Get At Least 10,000 High-Quality and Tailored Leads a Month

MAXIMIZE YOUR SOCIAL MEDIA REACH:
DOMINATE GOOGLE WITH TARGETED HASHTAGS AND KEYWORDS:

SEIZE THE MOMENT TO EXPAND YOUR INFLUENCE AND EMPOWER LIVES

magine harnessing the vast resources of Google's expansive public database, the precision of social media platforms, the reach of targeted hashtags, and the specificity of email lists to connect with individuals eager to embark on transformative journeys with you. Discover a treasure trove of clients and mentees who are not just seeking guidance but are ready to embrace profound change. Seize the moment, share your wisdom, and watch your influence expand! 🌟📷

Join the ranks of mentors, life coaches, and spiritual leaders who have already harnessed the transformative power of ATS Leads.

Unlock your capacity to empower lives with ATS Leads. Seize the moment and witness your influence soar.

Are you prepared to amplify your impact and inspire meaningful change? Experience the dynamic capabilities of ATS Leads today!

PHONE: (409)-457-6304

WEB: https://atsleads.net/

GLOBAL ECONOMIC OUTLOOK FOR 2024

NAVIGATING TRENDS, CHALLENGES AND OPPORTUNITIES

As we advance into 2024, the global economic landscape continues to evolve, influenced by a myriad of factors that promise to shape the future of trade, finance, and development. Understanding these dynamics is crucial for businesses, investors, and policymakers. Herein, we delve into an analytical exploration of the anticipated economic trends, challenges, and growth opportunities, offering expert insights into trade dynamics, inflation trajectories, and market predictions.

Emerging Economic Trends:

DIGITAL CURRENCY ADOPTION:

The increasing integration of digital currencies and blockchain technology within mainstream finance is expected to continue, potentially reshaping cross-border trade and payment systems. Experts predict a cautious but increasing acceptance of digital currencies, which could influence global trade patterns and monetary policies.

SUSTAINABILITY AND GREEN FINANCE:

With climate change ascending on the global agenda, sustainable investment is gaining traction. Green finance is anticipated to grow, driven by both ethical imperatives and economic incentives, as businesses and governments prioritize eco-friendly initiatives and investments in renewable energy.

TECHNOLOGICAL ADVANCEMENTS:

The relentless march of technology, particularly in AI, IoT, and big data, is poised to further disrupt industries, enhance productivity, and foster new economic opportunities. However, it also raises concerns about labor market shifts and the need for workforce reskilling.

ECONOMICS | TRIENT PRESS

Global Economic Challenges:

INEQUALITY AND SOCIAL UNREST:

Persistent inequality and inadequate economic recovery in certain sectors and regions could fuel social unrest, impacting market confidence and economic stability.

DEBT LEVELS:

Elevated government and corporate debt levels, exacerbated by the pandemic response, pose a risk to financial stability. Monitoring and managing these debt burdens, particularly in emerging economies, will be critical to averting fiscal crises.

GEOPOLITICAL TENSIONS:

Ongoing geopolitical conflicts and trade disputes remain a significant risk factor, with the potential to disrupt international supply chains, impact commodity prices, and stifle economic cooperation.

Expert Commentary:

Economists and market analysts underscore the importance of adaptability and vigilance. Businesses are advised to remain agile, diversifying their supply chains and investment portfolios to mitigate risks. Policymakers are encouraged to foster economic resilience through supportive regulatory frameworks, investment in infrastructure, and strategies to promote technological adoption and workforce development.

Growth Opportunities:

INNOVATION AND ENTREPRENEURSHIP:

Sectors such as biotechnology, renewable energy, and e-commerce are likely to see continued growth and innovation, offering investment opportunities and potential for economic diversification.

EMERGING MARKETS:

Despite global challenges, emerging markets could present robust growth opportunities, driven by youthful populations, increasing digitalization, and growing consumer markets. Companies and investors may find value in diversifying their exposure to these dynamic economies.

TRADE AGREEMENTS:

New or revised trade agreements could emerge as a response to the shifting geopolitical landscape, potentially creating new opportunities for cross-border commerce and economic collaboration.

In conclusion, while the global economic outlook for 2024 presents its share of uncertainties and challenges, it also offers avenues for growth and innovation. By staying informed and proactive, stakeholders across the spectrum can navigate the complexities of the global economy and capitalize on the opportunities that arise in an ever-changing economic landscape.

BRIDGING PERSONAL AND BUSINESS PROSPERITY

FOUNDATIONS OF FINANCIAL EMPOWERMENT

BRIDGING PERSONAL AND BUSINESS PROSPERITY

M.L. RUSCSAK

Trient Press®

FINANCIAL WELL-BEING: CULTIVATING YOUR ECONOMIC GARDEN

As we embrace the vitality of spring, a season synonymous with growth and renewal, it presents an apt metaphor for cultivating our financial well-being. Just as gardeners meticulously plan and nurture their gardens, individuals and businesses can apply similar diligence and foresight to foster their economic health. Here, we delve into strategies aimed at cultivating robust financial landscapes, focusing on nurturing growth, pruning debt, and sowing the seeds of smart financial planning.

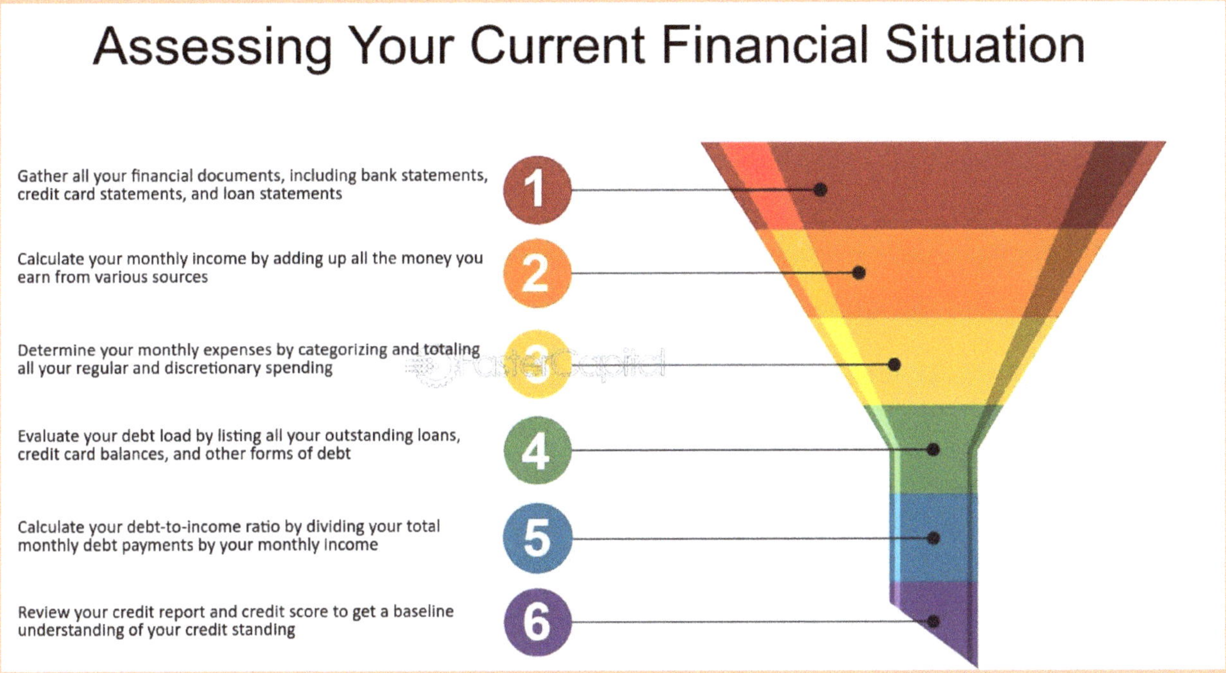

Assessing Your Current Financial Situation

1. Gather all your financial documents, including bank statements, credit card statements, and loan statements
2. Calculate your monthly income by adding up all the money you earn from various sources
3. Determine your monthly expenses by categorizing and totaling all your regular and discretionary spending
4. Evaluate your debt load by listing all your outstanding loans, credit card balances, and other forms of debt
5. Calculate your debt-to-income ratio by dividing your total monthly debt payments by your monthly income
6. Review your credit report and credit score to get a baseline understanding of your credit standing

TRIENT PRESS MAGAZINE APRIL/ MAY

FOR INDIVIDUALS

Assess and Nourish Your Financial Soil:

Begin with a thorough assessment of your financial situation. Review your income, expenses, debts, and savings. Understanding where you stand financially provides a solid foundation from which to grow. It's akin to testing the soil before planting; you need to know the conditions you're working with.

Prune Your Debt:

Just as excessive weeds can choke a garden, high levels of debt can stifle your financial growth. Focus on reducing your debt, starting with high-interest liabilities. Consider methods like the debt avalanche or snowball techniques, which can help streamline your debt reduction strategy and free up resources for future growth.

Cultivate a Savings Plan:

Savings are the seedlings of your financial garden. Allocate a portion of your income to savings each month, treating it as a non-negotiable expense. Over time, these savings can grow and provide financial stability and resources for future opportunities or emergencies.

Invest in Financial Education:

Enhancing your understanding of financial concepts and market conditions is like enriching the soil. The more you know, the better equipped you'll be to make informed decisions that promote financial well-being.

FOR BUSINESSES:

Evaluate Your Financial Landscape:

Businesses should conduct regular financial reviews assessing cash flow, profit margins, and operational costs. This analysis helps identify areas of strength and those requiring attention, informing strategic decisions that promote growth and sustainability.

Reduce Operational Weeds:

Just as a gardener removes weeds to prevent them from competing with desired plants, businesses should identify and cut unnecessary expenses that detract from profitability. Regularly reviewing and optimizing operational costs can help ensure that resources are focused on areas that drive growth and efficiency.

Diversify Revenue Streams:

In gardening, biodiversity can lead to a healthier and more resilient ecosystem. Similarly, businesses can benefit from diversifying their revenue sources. Exploring new markets, product lines, or service offerings can help mitigate risk and promote financial stability.

Plan for the Future:

Just as gardeners plan for different planting seasons, businesses should develop financial forecasts and budgets that account for various market conditions and growth phases. This planning enables businesses to allocate resources effectively, pursue strategic investments, and prepare for future challenges and opportunities.

IN SUMMARY, CULTIVATING FINANCIAL WELL-BEING REQUIRES INTENTION, DISCIPLINE, AND A FORWARD-LOOKING APPROACH, WHETHER FOR INDIVIDUALS OR BUSINESSES. BY ASSESSING YOUR CURRENT FINANCIAL SITUATION, REDUCING DEBT, FOSTERING SAVINGS OR REVENUE GROWTH, AND PLANNING STRATEGICALLY, YOU CAN NURTURE A FINANCIAL GARDEN THAT FLOURISHES, PROVIDING STABILITY, GROWTH, AND PROSPERITY WELL INTO THE FUTURE.

ECONOMICS |TRIENT PRESS

The Impact of Remote Work:

Urban Economies

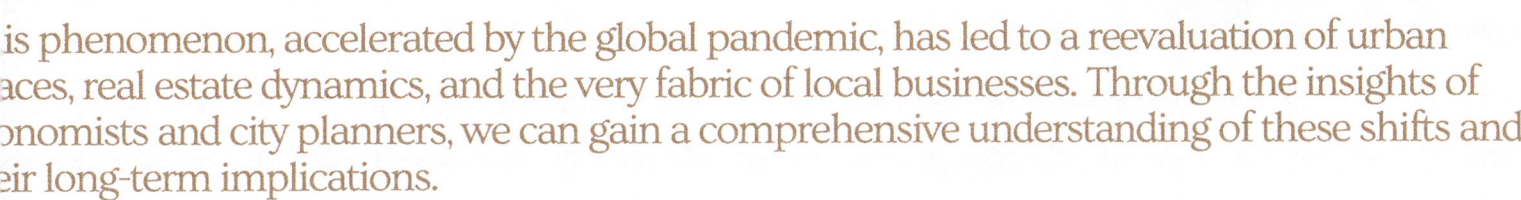

In recent years, the rise of remote work has precipitated a series of transformative shifts within urban economies across the globe. Once bustling city centers are undergoing changes as the traditional nine-to-five work model becomes increasingly decentralized.

This phenomenon, accelerated by the global pandemic, has led to a reevaluation of urban spaces, real estate dynamics, and the very fabric of local businesses. Through the insights of economists and city planners, we can gain a comprehensive understanding of these shifts and their long-term implications.

The migration of workers away from office-centric urban cores has had a pronounced effect on real estate markets. Commercial properties, particularly in central business districts, have witnessed reduced demand, prompting a reconsideration of their use and value. Concurrently, residential real estate in suburban and rural areas has seen an uptick as workers relocate to take advantage of lower living costs and enhanced quality of life, free from the constraints of daily commutes. This redistribution of population and economic activity is prompting a recalibration of urban planning priorities and real estate investment strategies.

ECONOMICS | TRIENT PRESS

Local businesses that once relied on heavy foot traffic and the patronage of office workers are adapting to this new reality. Retail outlets, restaurants, and service providers are diversifying their offerings and exploring digital engagemen strategies to attract a broader customer base beyond the immediate vicinity. Some urban centers are witnessing a shift toward more residential and mixed-use developments, aiming to create vibrant, self-sustaining communities that are less reliant on the influx of commuting workers.

Economists highlight the broader implications for urban economies, noting shifts in tax revenue bases and the potential for increased inequality between regions. Cities that were once magnets for talent and investment might need to reinvent themselves to remain competitive and attractive. This could involve investing in infrastructure, fostering innovation hubs, or enhancing quality of life factors to attract remote workers and new types of businesses.

City planners are contemplating these trends, recognizing the opportunity to redesign urban spaces for greater sustainability and resilience. There is a growing emphasis on creating '15-minute cities' where residents can access essential services and amenities within a short walk or bike ride from their homes, reducing dependence on cars and public transit. Such concepts not only address the challenges posed by the shift to remote work but also align with broader environmental and livability goals.

In conclusion, the impact of remote work on urban economies is multifaceted and ongoing. While it poses challenges to the traditional urban economic model, it also offers opportunities for innovation and transformation. By leveraging the insights of economists and city planners, cities can navigate these changes, adapting to create more diverse, resilient, and sustainable economies that are better equipped to thrive in the new landscape of work. As we look to the future, the ability of urban centers to evolve and respond to these dynamics will be a critical determinant of their success in the post-pandemic world.

GLOBAL ECONOMIC *Blossoming*

EMERGING MARKETS TO WATCH

In the intricate tapestry of the global economy, emerging markets stand out as vibrant threads, weaving patterns of growth and opportunity against the backdrop of the broader economic landscape. As we look towards a future marked by rapid technological advancements, demographic shifts, and evolving geopolitical dynamics, certain emerging markets are distinguishing themselves as beacons of potential and engines of economic blossoming.

Vietnamn:
With a young, dynamic workforce, strategic location in the heart of Southeast Asia, and a government committed to economic liberalization, Vietnam has emerged as a manufacturing and export powerhouse. The nation's focus on electronics, textiles, and agriculture, coupled with significant foreign direct investment, has propelled its economy forward. For businesses, engaging with Vietnam offers access to a burgeoning consumer market and a network of trade agreements that facilitate access to global markets.

India:
As one of the world's fastest-growing major economies, India presents a kaleidoscope of opportunities across sectors like technology, pharmaceuticals, and renewable energy. Its massive, tech-savvy youth population is driving innovation and digitalization, making India a hotbed for startups and tech companies. Businesses looking to engage with India can leverage its skilled labor force, burgeoning middle class, and policy reforms aimed at fostering entrepreneurship and investment.

Chile:

As a beacon of stability and innovation in Latin America, Chile boasts a robust economic foundation, underscored by its rich mineral resources, notably copper. Th country's commitment to sustainability, renewable energy, and technological adoptio presents opportunities in clean energy, mining, and agribusiness. Businesses can leverage Chile's transparent regulatory environment and focus on innovation to establish a foothold in Latin America.

As we consider these emerging markets, it is imperative to adopt a balanced perspective, recognizing not only the economic potential but also the contextual challenges. Effective engagement in these markets requires a deep understanding of local conditions, agile strategies to navigate economic fluctuations, and a commitment to sustainable practices that align with the broader goals of development and prosperity.

Engaging with these emerging markets requires a nuanced understanding of their unique cultural, economic, and regulatory landscapes. Building local partnerships, respecting local norms and practices, and contributing to sustainable development are key to fostering long-term relationships and unlocking mutual benefits. By tapping into the growth potential of these emerging economies, businesses can diversify their portfolios, drive global innovation, and participate in the economic blossoming that will shape the world's future.

Indonesia:

With its vast archipelago, abundant natural resources, and strategic position as a gateway to ASEAN markets, Indonesia is ripe for economic growth. The country's emphasis on infrastructure development and digital economy expansion, along with a large and young consumer base, makes it an attractive market for sectors ranging from e-commerce to renewable energy. By partnering with local firms and aligning with the government's development agenda, businesses can tap into Indonesia's growth trajectory.

Nigeria:

Africa's largest economy is poised for expansion across diverse sectors, from agriculture to fintech. Nigeria's youthful population, entrepreneurial spirit, and wealth of natural resources underpin its growth prospects. The burgeoning tech scene, particularly in Lagos, is a testament to the country's innovative potential. Businesses can engage with Nigeria by investing in its human capital, supporting sustainable practices, and contributing to the infrastructure that will underpin its future growth.

PATH BENDER

By: Antonio T. Smith, Jr

HARDCOVER PRICE: $29.99

FIGHTING FOR MY LIFE TO WIN (PAPERBACK)

By: Arshisa Adejiyan

PRICE: $16.99

OFF THE PATH (PAPERBACK)

By: Tierell Goodman

PRICE: $24.99

RESILIENT SAILING (PAPERBACK)

By: Dr Carl M Barnes

PRICE: $28.26

NATURE'S PHARMACY : UNLOCKING THE POWER OF MEDICINAL HERBS

By: Deaunna M Smith

PRICE: $32.99

ARE YOU HAPPY : FINDING THE CEO IN YOU (HARDCOVER)

By: M.L.Ruscsak

PRICE: $29.99

Embracing the Serenity: A moment of mindfulness in the midst of nature, brought to you by Trient Press – nurturing your mindset, one page at a time.

+1 -775-249-7401

info@trientperess.com
www.trientpress.com

"From Fear to Freedom, A Guide to Escaping Coercive Control" is a powerful and inspiring guide for survivors of coercive control. Written by M.L. Ruscsak, a survivor herself, this book provides comprehensive roadmap for healing and growth after experiencing the trauma of coercive control.

With a compassionate and empowering tone, Ruscsak draws on her own experiences and expe knowledge to help readers navigate the complexities of coercive control relationships, understand the impact of trauma on the mind and body, and develop effective coping strategi From redefining self and values to establishing healthy boundaries and relationships, from advocacy and activism to living a life of freedom and fulfillment, each chapter provides practica insights and exercises to help readers move forward with resilience and hope.

In addition to sharing her own story, Ruscsak includes the voices and experiences of other survivors, highlighting the diversity and strength of the survivor community. She also provides wealth of resources for additional support, including national and international organizations, books, and online communities.

"From Fear to Freedom" is a must-read for anyone who has experienced the trauma of coercive control, as well as for friends, family members, and professionals seeking to suppo survivors. With its clear and compassionate guidance, this book is a beacon of hope and healing for all those seeking to rise strong from the ashes of abuse."

AI Innovations & Their Impact on Industries

Trient Press Staff Writer

In the dynamic realm of technological advancement, artificial intelligence (AI) stands out as a transformative force, reshaping industries with unprecedented innovations. Across sectors such as healthcare, finance, and education, AI's impact is profound, driving efficiency, enhancing services, and unveiling new frontiers of possibility. By examining the latest breakthroughs in AI and exploring case studies across these pivotal industries, we can appreciate the breadth and depth of AI's transformative potential.

HEALTHCARE: REVOLUTIONIZING PATIENT CARE AND RESEARCH

In healthcare, AI is a game-changer, enhancing patient outcomes, streamlining diagnosis processes, and personalizing treatment plans. A notable breakthrough is the development of AI algorithms that can analyze medical images with precision surpassing human experts. For instance, Google Health's AI model can interpret mammograms to identify breast cancer with greater accuracy, reducing false positives and accelerating diagnosis.

Moreover, AI-powered predictive analytics are being deployed to anticipate patient risks and improve preventative care. An example is the deployment of AI systems in hospitals to predict patient deterioration hours before it would typically be identified by healthcare professionals. These systems analyze vast datasets, identifying subtle patterns that human observers might miss, enabling timely interventions and saving lives.

FINANCE: ENHANCING DECISION-MAKING AND FRAUD DETECTION

In finance, AI is reshaping operations, risk assessment, and customer service, providing institutions with powerful tools to enhance decision-making and security. Robo-advisors, utilizing AI algorithms, now offer personalized investment advice at a fraction of the cost of human financial advisors, democratizing access to financial planning.

AI's impact on fraud detection is particularly noteworthy, with systems now capable of analyzing transaction patterns in real-time to identify suspicious activities. For example, Mastercard employs AI to scrutinize each transaction across its network, assessing risk factors instantaneously to flag and prevent fraudulent transactions, thereby safeguarding consumer assets and trust.

EDUCATION: PERSONALIZING LEARNING AND EXPANDING ACCESS

In education, AI is breaking down traditional barriers and tailoring learning experiences to individual needs. AI-driven platforms can adapt in real time to a student's learning pace and style, offering customized resources and feedback. Carnegie Learning's MATHia, for instance, uses AI to provide real-time feedback and personalized learning paths in mathematics, demonstrating significant improvements in student outcomes.

Furthermore, AI is expanding access to education through intelligent tutoring systems and language translation applications, bridging geographic and linguistic divides. AI-powered tools like Duolingo offer language learning that adapts to individual proficiency levels, making education more accessible and engaging for users worldwide.

IN CONCLUSION

The infusion of AI across various sectors is just about technological prowess but represe a paradigm shift in how we approach proble and opportunities. In healthcare, finance, ar education, AI's potential to augment human ability, enhance efficiency, and unlock new insights is only beginning to be realized. As continue to explore and harness AI's capabilities, it is imperative to navigate ethic considerations, ensuring that these innovatio benefit society inclusively and equitably. Th journey of AI is one of the most exhilarating modern science and technology, promising t redefine our world in ways we are just beginning to imagine.

MICA BEAUTY

UNLEASH YOUR TRUE BEAUTY WITH MICABEAUTY - WHERE EVERY SHADE IS CELEBRATED!

Discover Your Perfect Match: Dive into the world of MicaBeauty, where we embrace every skin tone with our inclusive and personalized beauty range. From radiant foundations to luscious lip balms, our non-toxic, harsh chemical-free products are crafted for your unique beauty.

Be Part of Our Story: Join us on a journey of beauty that defies norms. At MicaBeauty, we're more than just a brand; we're a community that celebrates the real you.

https://shrsl.com/4cp62

GLOW GETTER VALUE KIT

$175.00 ~~$210.00~~

or 4 interest-free payments of $43.75 with afterpay

6-piece full size skincare products + mini fridge

Note: Kits are not available internationally

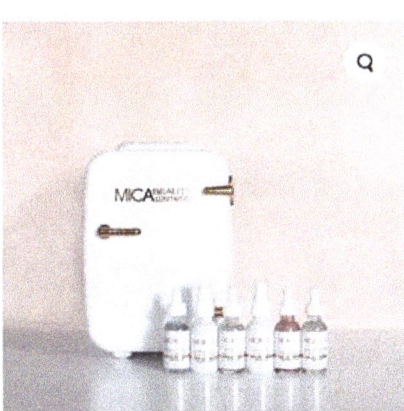
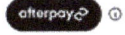

Special Offer: Enjoy free shipping on U.S. orders over $50! Plus, get a FREE mini fridge with purchases over $100*

FORTIFYING THE DIGITAL FRONTIER: STRATEGIC CYBERSECURITY IN THE CONTEMPORARY BUSINESS LANDSCAPE

In the intricate and interconnected realm of modern commerce, cybersecurity emerges as a paramount concern, underpinning the integrity and resilience of businesses in the digital age. As enterprises increasingly migrate their operations, assets, and data online, the imperative to safeguard these digital resources against ever-evolving threats has never been more acute. This article delineates the critical importance of cybersecurity, elucidates common online threats that businesses encounter, and delineates best practices for fortifying digital defenses.

The quintessence of cybersecurity in today's business context cannot be overstated. With the digital transformation accelerating across sectors, companies are amassing vast repositories of data and relying on complex digital systems for their core operations. This digitization, while driving efficiency and innovation, also expands the attack surface for malicious actors intent on exploiting vulnerabilities for financial gain, espionage, or sabotage.

Businesses today grapple with a gamut of cybersecurity threats, from sophisticated phishing schemes and ransomware attacks to insider threats and state-sponsored hacking. Phishing attacks, for instance, employ deceptive communications to trick employees into divulging sensitive information or granting access to secure systems. Ransomware, another pervasive threat, involves the encryption of a company's data by hackers, who then demand payment for its release. Insider threats, meanwhile, arise from within the organization, involving employees who, whether inadvertently or with malice, compromise security protocols or leak data.

TECHNOLOGY | TRIENT PRESS

To navigate this fraught landscape, businesses must adopt a multifaceted cybersecurity strategy, anchored in robust policies, cutting-edge technologies, and a culture of vigilance. Key best practices include:

- Comprehensive Risk Assessments: Regularly evaluating the organization's digital assets, identifying potential vulnerabilities, and assessing the risk profile to prioritize security measures.

- Employee Training and Awareness: Cultivating a cybersecurity-aware workforce through ongoing education on potential threats and best practices, ensuring employees are the first line of defense against attacks.

- Adopting Advanced Security Technologies: Implementing state-of-the-art cybersecurity solutions, including firewalls, anti-malware software, encryption, and intrusion detection systems, to safeguard against and respond to threats dynamically.

- Incident Response Planning: Developing and regularly updating an incident response plan to ensure swift and coordinated action in the event of a security breach, minimizing damage and facilitating recovery.

- Compliance and Collaboration: Adhering to relevant legal and regulatory standards governing data protection and cybersecurity, and engaging in industry collaboration to share insights and best practices.

As the digital economy burgeons and cyber threats proliferate, the onus is squarely on businesses to elevate their cybersecurity posture. By understanding the landscape of digital threats, implementing rigorous security protocols, and fostering a culture of cyber awareness, businesses can safeguard their digital assets and fortify their position in the digital age. The journey toward robust cybersecurity is continuous and necessitates a strategic, informed approach to navigate the complexities of the modern digital milieu.

TRIENT PRESS MAGAZINE APRIL/ MAY

Innovative Horizons

San Diego's Tech Entrepreneurs Catalyzing Growth

Nestled within the vibrant landscape of California, San Diego emerges not only as a picturesque coastal city but also as a burgeoning epicenter for technological innovation and entrepreneurial vigor. The city's unique confluence of academic institutions, research centers, and a collaborative business ecosystem provides fertile ground for tech-driven growth. This article explores how San Diego's tech entrepreneurs are harnessing new technologies to spur business expansion and innovation, propelling the city into the limelight as a crucible of technological advancement.

San Diego's tech scene is distinguished by its diversity, spanning biotechnology, telecommunications, software development, and clean tech, among other sectors. Entrepreneurs in the region are adept at leveraging the city's robust infrastructure and supportive networks to pilot and scale their innovations. Notable among these is the proliferation of startups that are venturing into the realms of artificial intelligence (AI), blockchain, and the Internet of Things (IoT), reflecting broader trends in the tech industry.

In the domain of biotechnology, San Diego's entrepreneurs are making groundbreaking strides, utilizing AI to accelerate drug discovery and personalize medical treatments. By harnessing AI's data-processing capabilities, these innovators are decoding complex biological data at unprecedented speeds, expediting the development of life-saving therapies and bringing them to market with enhanced efficiency.

The telecommunications sector in San Diego is similarly thriving, with local entrepreneurs deploying advanced technologies to bolster connectivity and foster digital inclusion. Initiatives leveraging 5G technology exemplify this trend, offering transformative prospects for enhanced internet speed, lower latency, and the enablement of next-generation applications in healthcare, education, and public safety.

Furthermore, the software industry in San Diego is a hotbed of innovation, with entrepreneurs developing cutting-edge applications that cater to diverse market needs.

> "From cybersecurity solutions to predictive analytics and enterprise software, these technological advancements are driving business efficiencies, enhancing customer experiences, and fostering economic growth."

Clean tech represents another vibrant sector where San Diego's tech entrepreneurs are making significant inroads. Leveraging technologies like blockchain, they are developing sustainable energy solutions that promote environmental stewardship while addressing market demands. These initiatives not only contribute to the city's green economy but also position San Diego as a leader in sustainable technological innovation.

In conclusion, San Diego's tech entrepreneurs are at the forefront of harnessing new technologies to drive business growth and innovation. Their ventures reflect a deep-seated culture of creativity, collaboration, and resilience, propelling the city to the forefront of the global tech landscape. As they continue to break new ground and redefine industry paradigms, San Diego's tech entrepreneurs embody the spirit of innovation, underscoring the city's status as a crucible of technological progress and economic dynamism.

TRIENT PRESS MAGAZINE — APRIL/ MAY

Quantum Horizons:
Unveiling the Future Through Quantum Computing

Trient Press Staff Writer

As a tech engineer deeply entrenched in the evolving landscape of computational technologies, I have witnessed firsthand the burgeoning rise of quantum computing—a field that promises to redefine the boundaries of data processing and problem-solving. This groundbreaking advancement stands poised to revolutionize multiple sectors by harnessing the principles of quantum mechanics, offering computational power that dwarfs that of even the most advanced classical computers.

At its core, quantum computing diverges fundamentally from classical computing through its use of quantum bits, or qubits. Unlike classical bits, which are confined to a state of either 0 or 1, qubits can exist in multiple states simultaneously, thanks to the phenomena of superposition and entanglement. This attribute allows quantum computers to process vast datasets and perform complex calculations at speeds unattainable by their classical counterparts, heralding a new era of computational efficiency and capability.

The potential applications of quantum computing are as vast and varied as they are transformative. In the realm of cryptography, quantum computers could crack codes that are currently deemed unbreakable, necessitating a reimagining of data security protocols. Pharmaceutical companies stand to benefit immensely, as quantum computing can significantly expedite the drug discovery process by simulating molecular interactions at an unprecedented scale and speed. Moreover, in the field of artificial intelligence, the integration of quantum computing promises to accelerate the development of AI systems, enabling them to solve intricate problems with greater nuance and precision.

However, the ascent of quantum computing also presents an array of challenges and considerations. The hardware required to stabilize and read qubits is exceedingly complex, necessitating environments with extreme temperatures close to absolute zero. Additionally, the nascent nature of quantum algorithms means there is still much to learn and refine in harnessing the full potential of this technology.

Despite these hurdles, the momentum behind quantum computing continues to build, driven by both public and private sector investments and a growing recognition of its transformative potential. As we stand on the cusp of this technological leap, it is imperative for tech professionals, policymakers, and the broader public to engage with and understand the implications of quantum computing. By doing so, we can collectively navigate the ethical and practical challenges it poses, ensuring that this potent technology serves to enhance and not undermine the societal good.

The rise of quantum computing marks a pivotal chapter in the story of technological progress, one that embodies both immense promise and significant challenges. As tech engineers and as a society, our task is to steward this powerful tool with wisdom, foresight, and a keen awareness of its broader impacts, ensuring that its integration into our digital infrastructure heralds a future replete with opportunity and innovation.

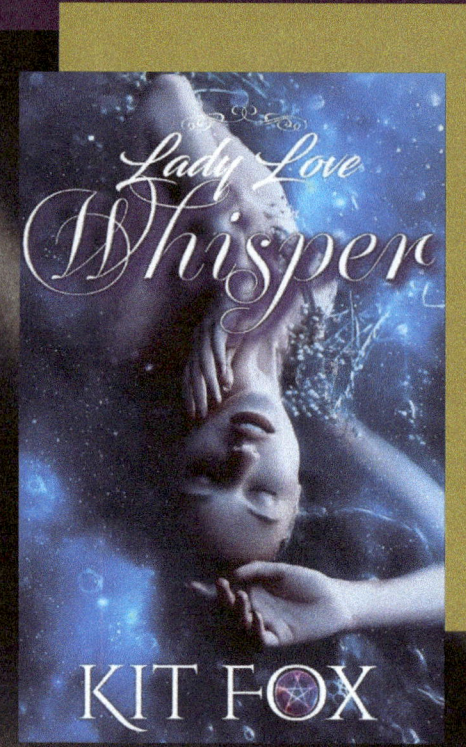

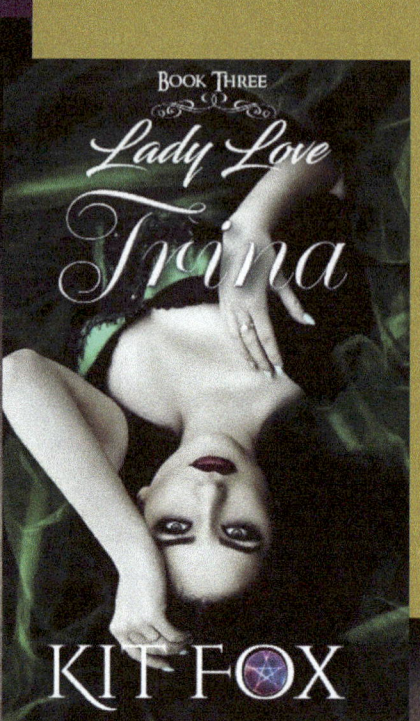

Kit Fox

Traveling with Trient

TRAVEL TIPS
AND A TASTE OF THE CITY

WWW.TRIENTPRESSMAGAZINE.COM

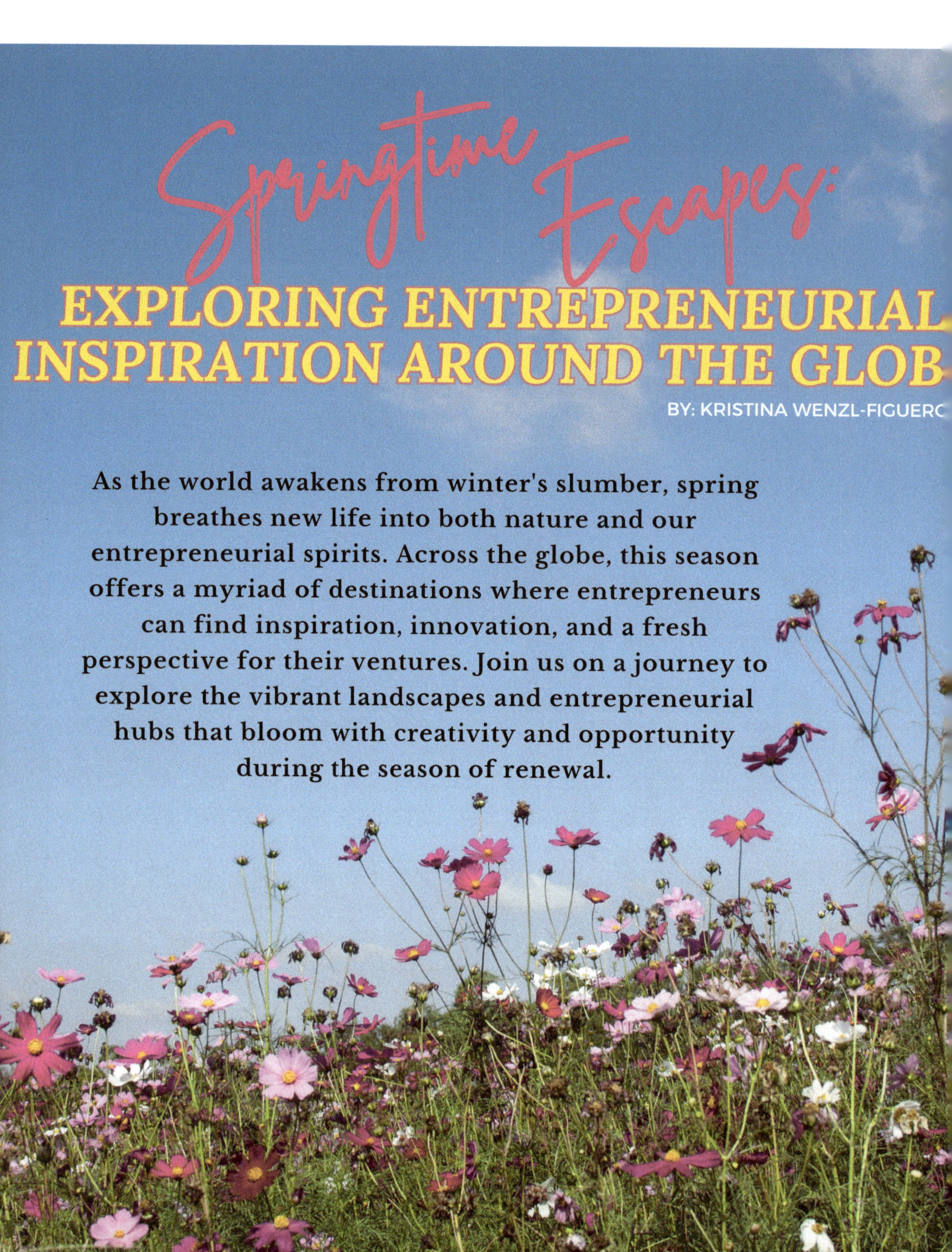

Springtime Escapes:
EXPLORING ENTREPRENEURIAL INSPIRATION AROUND THE GLOB

BY: KRISTINA WENZL-FIGUERC

As the world awakens from winter's slumber, spring breathes new life into both nature and our entrepreneurial spirits. Across the globe, this season offers a myriad of destinations where entrepreneurs can find inspiration, innovation, and a fresh perspective for their ventures. Join us on a journey to explore the vibrant landscapes and entrepreneurial hubs that bloom with creativity and opportunity during the season of renewal.

Destination 1:
Kyoto, Japan -
Cherry Blossom Serenity Meets Entrepreneurial Zen

In Kyoto, Japan, springtime transforms the city into a mesmerizing sea of pink as cherry blossoms blanket the landscape. Amidst this ethereal beauty, entrepreneurs find inspiration in the city's rich cultural heritage and entrepreneurial ethos. From traditional tea ceremonies to modern tech startups, Kyoto's blend of serenity and innovation offers a unique perspective on balancing tradition with progress.

Destination 2:
Silicon Valley, California -
Where Innovation Springs Eternal

No list of entrepreneurial destinations would be complete without a visit to Silicon Valley, the epicenter of technological innovation. In spring, the valley's lush landscapes provide a picturesque backdrop for brainstorming sessions and outdoor networking events. Here, entrepreneurs can immerse themselves in a culture of disruption and creativity, drawing inspiration from the trailblazers who have shaped the future of technology.

Destination 3:
Amsterdam, Netherlands -
Tulip Mania and the Spirit of Entrepreneurship

As tulips bloom across the Netherlands, Amsterdam bursts with entrepreneurial energy and creativity. From its bustling startup scene to its vibrant arts and culture, the city offers a dynamic environment for entrepreneurs to thrive. Whether strolling along the canals or attending networking events in historic buildings, springtime in Amsterdam ignites the entrepreneurial spirit and fosters new connections and ideas.

Destination 4:
Cape Town, South Africa -
Springtime Innovation at the Gateway to Africa

In Cape Town, spring brings a sense of renewal and possibility to Africa's entrepreneurial capital. Against the backdrop of Table Mountain and the Atlantic Ocean, entrepreneurs gather to collaborate, innovate, and explore new opportunities. With its diverse community and vibrant startup ecosystem, Cape Town offers a gateway to the continent's burgeoning markets and untapped potential.

As entrepreneurs, we are constantly seeking new sources of inspiration and innovation to fuel our ventures. This spring, why not embark on a journey to discover the world's most inspiring entrepreneurial destinations? From the cherry blossom-lined streets of Kyoto to the tech hubs of Silicon Valley, the possibilities for springtime exploration are endless. So pack your bags, embrace the spirit of adventure, and let the season of renewal inspire your next entrepreneurial breakthrough.

TRAVEL |TRIENT PRESS

TRIENT PRESS MAGAZINE APRIL/ MAY

DISCOVERING ENTREPRENEURIAL SPRING:

A Journey of Innovation and Inspiration

BY KRISTINA WENZL-FIGUEROA

As travelers eagerly anticipate the thawing of winter's grip, there's an undeniable sense of anticipation in the air. Spring heralds a time of rejuvenation and renewal, a season where the world bursts forth in a kaleidoscope of colors and scents. But beyond its natural beauty, spring holds a special allure for entrepreneurs seeking inspiration and innovation.

"Springtime is nature's way of inviting us to step outside and explore its wonders."
— Anonymous

For entrepreneurs with a penchant for adventure, the season beckons with the promise of new beginnings and fresh opportunities. Just as travelers embark on journeys to discover hidden gems and breathtaking landscapes, entrepreneurs set out to chart their own paths to success.

TRAVEL | TRIENT PRESS

TRIENT PRESS MAGAZINE　　　　　　　　　APRIL/ MAY

Embracing Change in Entrepreneurial Escapes

In the realm of entrepreneurship, spring is a time of exploration and discovery. Just as travelers immerse themselves in the culture and beauty of distant lands, entrepreneurs immerse themselves in the endless possibilities of their ventures.

"To travel is to take a journey into yourself."
— Danny Kaye

Successful entrepreneurs understand that the journey to success is often as rewarding as the destination itself. Whether it's venturing into uncharted markets or forging new partnerships, springtime inspires a sense of adventure and a willingness to embrace the unknown.

Seizing Opportunities Amidst Scenic Splendor

Spring is a season of surprises, where hidden treasures lie waiting to be uncovered. For entrepreneurs, this means seizing upon opportunities that may have been overlooked during the colder months.

"The world is full of magic things, patiently waiting for our senses to grow sharper." — *W.B. Yeats*

TRAVEL | TRIENT PRESS

Just as travelers stumble upon hidden gems off the beaten path, entrepreneurs stumble upon innovative ideas and untapped markets that hold the potential for success. By keeping their senses attuned to the ever-changing landscape of business, entrepreneurs can uncover hidden treasures that propel their ventures to new heights.

Capturing the Essence of Entrepreneurial Spring

More than just a season, spring is a state of mind—a time to embrace the vibrancy and vitality of life. For entrepreneurs, this means capturing the essence of spring in their endeavors and infusing their ventures with the same sense of renewal and growth.

"Spring is the time of plans and projects." - Leo Tolstoy

From launching new products to revamping marketing strategies, spring inspires entrepreneurs to breathe new life into their businesses and embark on bold new endeavors. Just as travelers return from their journeys with tales of adventure and discovery, entrepreneurs emerge from the spring season with stories of innovation and success.

TRIENT PRESS MAGAZINE　　　　　　　　　APRIL/ MAY

Entrepreneurial Escapes: Insights from Inspirational Traveler

Among those who have ventured into the realm of entrepreneurial spring is Sarah Blake, founder of a sustainable fashion brand. Drawing inspiration from the season's regenerative qualities, Sarah has built a business that reflects her commitment to environmental stewardship.

"Spring reminds us of the importance of sustainability and renewal. Through our brand, we strive to create fashion that not only looks good but also does good for the planet." - Sarah Blake

Similarly, John Smith, CEO of a tech startup, attributes much of his company's success to the spirit of innovation fostered by the season.

"Springtime invigorates our team with a sense of possibility and creativity. It's a time when we're inspired to push the boundaries of what's possible and redefine the future of technology." - John Smith

Conclusion: Embark on Your Entrepreneurial Spring Adventure

As travelers embark on journeys to explore the wonders of the world, entrepreneurs embark on journeys to explore the possibilities of their ventures. In the season of spring, where innovation blooms and opportunities abound, entrepreneurs find inspiration in the beauty and vitality of the world around them. By embracing the spirit of exploration, seizing upon hidden treasures, and capturing the essence of spring in their endeavors, entrepreneurs can embark on a journey of discovery that leads to unparalleled success. So pack your bags, embrace the spirit of entrepreneurial spring, and set out on an adventure that will ignite your creativity, fuel your passion, and redefine the landscape of entrepreneurship.

TRAVEL |TRIENT PRESS

Unveiling Spring's Hidden Gems:

Quirky Destinations for the Adventurous Traveler

BY: KRISTINA WENZL-FIGUEROA

Spring is a time of rebirth, and what better way to celebrate than by uncovering the offbeat charms of destinations that come alive in this whimsical season? From secret gardens tucked away in bustling cities to eccentric festivals that defy convention, these quirky spring destinations promise an unforgettable journey for the adventurous traveler.

TRAVEL | TRIENT PRESS

Japan

Hitachi Seaside Park, Japan: The Flower Carpet Phenomenon

Nestled along the coast of Ibaraki Prefecture lies a botanical wonderland unlike any other. During spring, Hitachi Seaside Park transforms into a kaleidoscope of colors as millions of baby blue eyes flowers carpet the landscape. This breathtaking phenomenon, known as the "Nemophila Harmony," draws visitors from far and wide to wander through fields of blue beneath the clear spring sky. Don't miss the chance to capture Instagram-worthy shots amidst this enchanting sea of flowers.

TRAVEL | TRIENT PRESS

TRIENT PRESS MAGAZINE APRIL/ MAY

Belgium

Hallerbos Forest in Halle, Belgium: The Enchanted Blue Forest

Hidden within the heart of Belgium lies a forest straight out of a fairy tale. Every spring, the Hallerbos comes alive with a carpet of bluebells, blanketing the forest floor in a mesmerizing hue of purple-blue. Follow winding trails through this enchanted woodland as sunlight filters through the canopy, casting dappled shadows on the forest floor. For photographers and nature enthusiasts alike, Hallerbos offers a magical escape from the ordinary.

TRAVEL |TRIENT PRESS

TRIENT PRESS MAGAZINE   APRIL/ MAY

Turkey

Cappadocia, Turkey: Hot Air Balloons Over Blossoming Valleys

While Cappadocia is famous for its otherworldly landscapes and fairy chimneys, spring brings an added layer of enchantment to this captivating region. As winter gives way to warmer temperatures, the valleys of Cappadocia burst into bloom with wildflowers, creating a stunning contrast against the rugged terrain. Experience the beauty of spring from a unique vantage point by soaring high above the valleys in a hot air balloon. Drift serenely amidst the blossoms as the sun rises, painting the sky with hues of gold and pink.

TRAVEL |TRIENT PRESS

TRIENT PRESS MAGAZINE   APRIL/ MAY

China

Harbin, China: Ice Melting Festival

While most people associate spring with thawing snow and blooming flowers, Harbin, China, celebrates the season in a truly unconventional way. Each year, as winter bids farewell, the city hosts the Ice Melting Festival, a quirky event that marks the transition from icy cold to springtime warmth.

Watch in awe as intricate ice sculptures crafted during the winter months gradually melt away under the spring sun, transforming into ephemeral works of art. Join locals in festive celebrations featuring traditional music, dance, and culinary delights, making the Ice Melting Festival a one-of-a-kind springtime spectacle.

TRAVEL |TRIENT PRESS

TRIENT PRESS MAGAZINE　　　　　　　　　　　　　　APRIL/ MAY

Songkran, Thailand
World's Biggest Water Fight

Northern India
Holi ~Festival of Color

Embrace the Quirkiness of Spring

As spring breathes new life into the world, it also unveils hidden treasures and eccentric delights waiting to be discovered by intrepid travelers.

Whether you're wandering through a sea of bluebells in Belgium, floating above blossoming valleys in Turkey, or witnessing the melting of ice sculptures in China, these quirky spring destinations offer an escape from the ordinary and a chance to embrace the whimsical side of travel.

So venture off the beaten path, embrace the quirkiness of spring, and let your adventures unfold in unexpected ways.

TRAVEL | TRIENT PRESS

TRIENT PRESS MAGAZINE　　　　　　　　　　　　APRIL/ MAY

Run for the Roses:

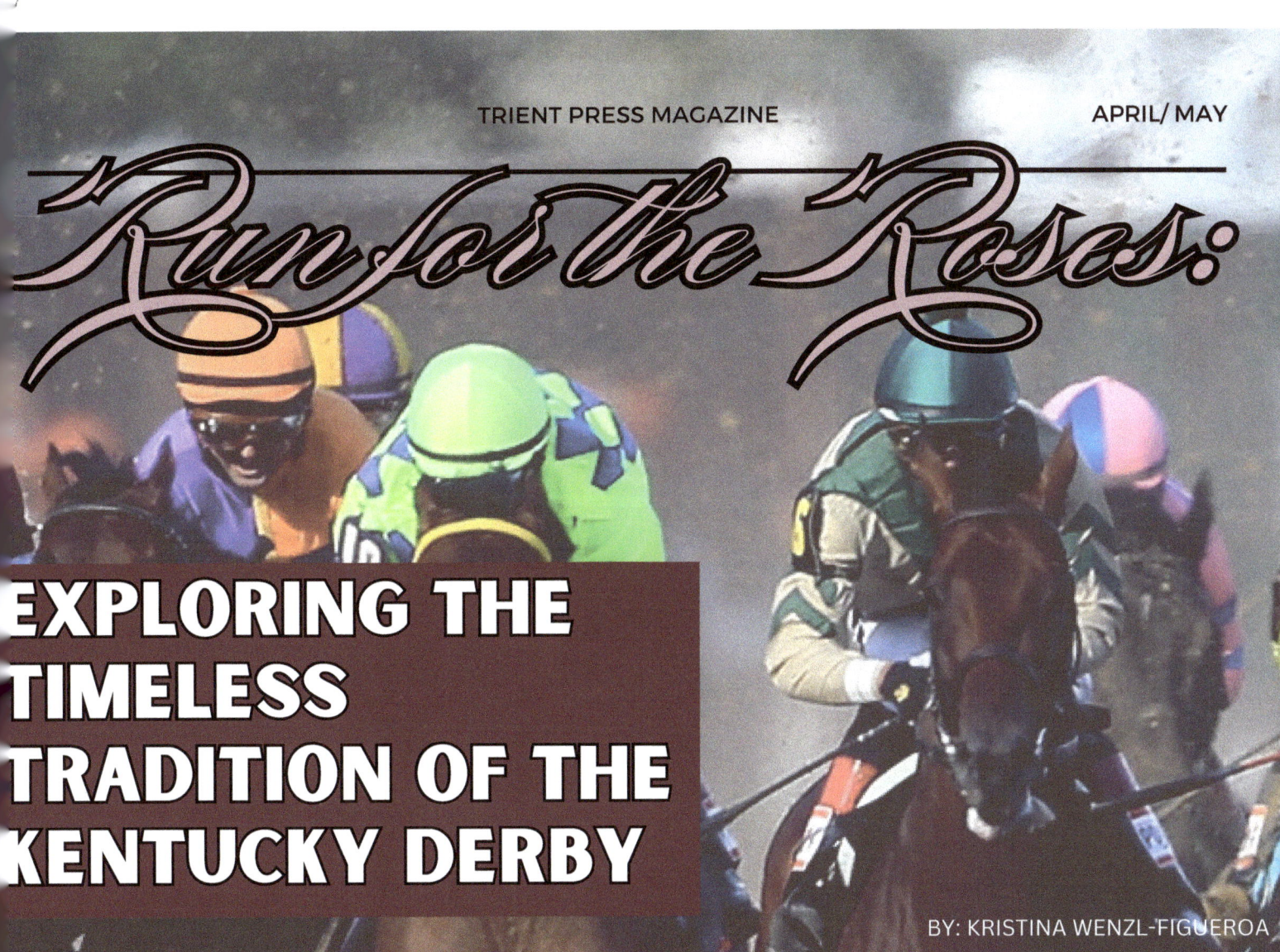

EXPLORING THE TIMELESS TRADITION OF THE KENTUCKY DERBY

BY: KRISTINA WENZL-FIGUEROA

As spring blooms across the United States, there's one event that captures the hearts and imaginations of millions: the Kentucky Derby. Held annually on the first Saturday in May at Churchill Downs in Louisville, Kentucky, the Derby is more than just a horse race—it's a celebration of Southern culture, fashion, and the enduring spirit of tradition. Join us as we delve into the rich history and timeless allure of the "Run for the Roses."

A Legacy of Excellence

Since its inception in 1875, the Kentucky Derby has stood as a symbol of excellence in horse racing. Known as the "Most Exciting Two Minutes in Sports," the Derby attracts top thoroughbred horses from around the world, all vying for a chance to etch their names into the annals of racing history. From the thunderous roar of hooves on the track to the electric atmosphere of the grandstands, the Derby is a spectacle unlike any other.

Southern Hospitality and Style

But the Kentucky Derby is about more than just horse racing—it's a showcase of Southern hospitality and style. Attendees come dressed to the nines in their finest attire, with women donning colorful sundresses and elaborate hats, and men sporting seersucker suits and bow ties. From the infield to Millionaires Row, the Derby is a fashion extravaganza where every attendee becomes part of the spectacle.

Mint Juleps and Culinary Delights

No Derby experience would be complete without indulging in the quintessential Southern libation: the mint julep. Made with Kentucky bourbon, fresh mint, sugar, and crushed ice, the mint julep is as much a part of Derby tradition as the race itself. Pair your julep with Southern delicacies like hot browns, bourbon balls, and Derby pie for a culinary journey through the flavors of the South.

"At the Kentucky Derby, the spectacle unfolds: where fashion meets tradition, and thundering hooves echo the pulse of excitement."

TRAVEL | TRIENT PRESS

The Kentucky Derby: a timeless tradition, a legendary race.

Beyond the Track: Festivities and Fanfare

While the main event is undoubtedly the race itself, the Kentucky Derby offers a plethora of festivities and fanfare to enjoy throughout Derby Week. From the Kentucky Oaks, a premier race for three-year-old fillies held the day before the Derby, to the Pegasus Parade, a beloved Louisville tradition featuring floats, marching bands, and celebrity guests, there's something for everyone to enjoy leading up to the big race day.

Experience the Magic of the Kentucky Derby

As May blooms across the United States, the Kentucky Derby stands as a timeless tradition that continues to captivate and inspire. Whether you're a seasoned racing aficionado or a first-time attendee, the Derby offers an unparalleled experience that celebrates the best of Southern culture, fashion, and hospitality. So don your finest attire, sip on a mint julep, and join in the excitement of the "Run for the Roses"—an event that embodies the spirit of spring and the thrill of horse racing at its finest.

Kentucky Derby Mint Julep

Perfect for Derby Day or any other warm day, this cool and refreshing mint julep recipe is made with crushed ice, Kentucky bourbon and fresh mint.

INGREDIENTS

- 4-5 fresh mint leaves, roughly torn
- 1/2 - 1 oz simple syrup (recipe below in recipe notes) adjust per your tastes
- crushed ice
- splash of cold water
- 2 oz bourbon
- sprig of fresh mint (for garnish - optional)

DIRECTIONS

- To bottom of serving glass, add mint leaves and simple syrup. Muddle together with a muddler or handle of a wooden spoon.
- Top with plenty of crushed ice, then pour in splash of cold water, and bourbon.
- Stir, garnish with the sprig of mint, and serve!

SIMPLE SYRUP RECIPE

- 1 cup water
- 1 1/4 cup granulated sugar. Add water and sugar to small saucepan. Bring to a boil, stirring occasionally until sugar dissolves, boiling about 2 minutes. Remove from heat and let cool completely.

** makes more than needed for this recipe, but leftovers can be kept refrigerated 1-2 weeks **

HOW TO MAKE A MINT JULEP

1. Prepare simple syrup. This is best done ahead of time. It needs to be cooled when you add it to your cocktail. The good news is, a simple syrup can be refrigerated for up to 2 weeks, so feel free to make it as early as you need to.
2. Add mint and simple syrup to glass and muddle. Muddle is a fancy term for mashing together, so the flavors are "muddled" and not distinctive anymore. You can use a cocktail muddler or the handle of a wooden spoon, and just press down to sort of mash the mint into the syrup.
3. Add plenty of crushed ice. Almost all the way up to the top of the glass. If it mounds over a little, that's totally fine too. You want A LOT of ice.
4. Pour in water and bourbon. Don't worry, you're not watering down the bourbon, it's just a splash of water to help take some of the bite and burn out of a solid 2 oz of bourbon.
5. Stir, garnish, and serve.

VARIATIONS OF THIS RECIPE

- NON-ALCOHOLIC – There's really no way to make a non-alcoholic mint julep taste the same as a regular one, since bourbon has a distinctive taste. But here's how to make a mint julep that's beautiful, yet alcohol-free:
  - When making the simple syrup, add a splash of lemon juice
  - Replace bourbon with ginger ale

- SIMPLE SYRUP ALTERNATIVE – If a simple syrup isn't possible, add some granulated sugar to the mint and muddle (just as you would with the syrup). I definitely prefer the syrup though, since sugar can make the drink a bit grainy.

TRAVEL |TRIENT PRESS

OBBY FLAY'S Kentucky HOT BROWN

Star chef Bobby Flay smothers an open-face turkey sandwich with cheese sauce and bacon for his version of the over-the-top Louisville classic.

INGREDIENTS

SAUCE
2 1/4 CUPS WHOLE MILK
2 TABLESPOONS UNSALTED BUTTER
2 TABLESPOONS ALL-PURPOSE FLOUR
2 CUPS SHARP WHITE CHEDDAR CHEESE, SHREDDED (6 OUNCES)
1/4 CUP FRESHLY GRATED PARMIGIANO-REGGIANO CHEESE
PINCH OF FRESHLY GRATED NUTMEG
FEW DASHES OF HOT SAUCE
KOSHER SALT
FRESHLY GROUND BLACK PEPPER

SANDWICHES
16 SLICES OF THICK-CUT BACON
2 TOMATOES, CUT INTO 8 (1/4-INCH-THICK) SLICES
1 TABLESPOON CANOLA OIL
KOSHER SALT
FRESHLY GROUND BLACK PEPPER
8 (1/2-INCH-THICK) SLICES OF DAY-OLD WHITE SANDWICH BREAD
4 TABLESPOONS UNSALTED BUTTER, CUT INTO PIECES
2 POUNDS ROAST TURKEY BREAST, SLICED 1/4-INCH THICK
1 1/2 CUPS SHARP WHITE CHEDDAR CHEESE, SHREDDED (4 1/2 OUNCES)
1/2 CUP FRESHLY GRATED PARMIGIANO-REGGIANO CHEESE
CHOPPED CHIVES, FOR GARNISH
CHOPPED PARSLEY, FOR GARNISH

DIRECTIONS

Make the sauce

- In a small saucepan, bring the milk to a simmer. In a medium saucepan, melt the butter. Add the flour and whisk over moderate heat for 1 minute. Gradually whisk in the hot milk and bring to a boil. Cook, whisking, until thickened, about 5 minutes. Remove the pan from the heat and whisk in both cheeses until melted. Stir in the nutmeg and hot sauce and season with salt and pepper.

Make the sandwiches

- Preheat the oven to 425°F. Arrange the bacon on a rack set over a baking sheet. Cook until golden and crisp, about 30 minutes.
- Preheat the broiler. Arrange the tomato slices on a baking sheet, drizzle with the oil, and season with salt and pepper. Broil 6 inches from the heat until lightly charred, 1 to 2 minutes per side; keep warm.
- Arrange the bread on a foil-lined baking sheet and spread each slice with 1/2 tablespoon of the butter; season with salt and pepper. Broil until lightly toasted, about 2 minutes. Flip the bread and toast for 1 minute. Top each toast with some turkey and a slice of tomato. Spoon the sauce on top and sprinkle on both cheeses. Broil until the cheese is melted and golden brown, 2 to 3 minutes. Transfer the sandwiches to plates and top with the bacon. Garnish with chopped chives and parsley and serve hot.

Originally appeared: December 2015 Food & Wine

www.ingramcontent.com/pod-product-compliance
Lightning Source LLC
LaVergne TN
LVHW071637080526
838199LV00095BA/6737